# 7-7

# The London Bombs

## What Went Wrong?

GIBSON SQUARE

This edition first published in 2005 by

Printed on Munken Bookwove
Typeset in Bembo

Gibson Square Books Ltd
15 Gibson Square, London N1 0RD
Tel: +44 (0)20 7689 4790; Fax: +44 (0)20 7689 7395
publicity@gibsonsquare.com
www.gibsonsquare.com

UK & Ireland sales by Signature
20 Castlegate, York YO1 9RP
Tel 01904 633 633; Fax 01904 675 445
sales@signaturebooks.co.uk

UK & European distribution by Central Books Ltd
99 Wallis Road, UK London E9 5LN
Tel +44 (0)845 458 9911; Fax +44 (0)845 458 9912
info@centralbooks.com
www.centralbooks.com

Australian, New Zealand, Canada, South Africa, US sales,
please contact Gibson Square Books Ltd.

ISBN 1-903933-71-4

# Contents

# Foreword

The 7 July bombs seemed to have trapped us in the worst of both worlds. Many of those in charge of our security had been preaching the inevitability of an attack for months, and yet when it came they appear to have been taken by surprise.

The best way to prevent the recurrence of terrorism in our major cities is to carry out a hard-headed review of how the relevant government agencies performed in the run up to the attacks—not in private (impossible in any case because of the range of issues involved), but a vigorous public debate. Terrorists are ruthless and we must be ruthless in examining our national performance if we are to make it harder for them to strike.

Experiencing and analysing (often on the hoof) the events of 7 July and later 21 July, I experienced anger and humiliation that such low-level gangs had managed to outwit our security and intelligence services. When starting this book I thought I might find an answer in how we structured our security system or collected our intelligence. My targets would be institutions. Fix this or that part of the system: most notably MI5's Joint Terrorism Analysis Centre—which 'analyses all intelligence relating to international terrorism, at home and overseas' and 'produces assessments of threats and other terrorist-related subjects'—whose reduction of the threat state just five weeks before 7 July helped take our eye off the ball.

The system does need fixing, but my real targets have turned out to be ideas, mindsets and ways of looking at things, which appear to permeate not only our intelligence and security apparatus but also our national life. And which make it easier for terrorists to exist unhindered in our midst and more difficult for the police and security services to do their job. These ideas may in part be imposed from above, but generally are so dangerous not because anyone has to subscribe to them but because many people do—naturally.

Simply put, we have a bad and confused attitude to terrorism. If we do not make immediate efforts to level the playing field on which terrorists have to operate—the next bomb plots will be as easy to carry out as the last.

# Thursday 7 July 2005

Not since the 500lbs bombs slammed into the RFA Sir Galahad during the Falklands War had I been so close to death on a large scale. I was two hundred and fifty yards from the Tavistock Square bomb and a few hundred feet from Russell Square tube station.

We had known something was wrong straight away when the television reported power surges on the tube across London. It was not good news. 'Power surges' sounded suspiciously like a codename for a serious emergency on the tube line. I was uneasy to say the least. Then some minutes later we heard a detonation—muffled but distinct.

I had certainly been bombed before—by the Argentine Naval Air force in their daring attacks on the landing ships at Bluff Cove in 1982—and I had heard bombs going off in Belfast in the mid 1980s.

This bomb was nearby, but there was no concussion or shock wave and no windows broken—so it was small. It was a Belfast-type bomb rather than anything more dramatic. Small and possibly very nasty, but not on a grand scale. As we were certain it was a bomb, the 'power surges' were probably bombs too.

I can't say that I was ever especially frightened in the Falklands, even when the bombs were raining down. But that was different. I was young and a professional soldier, and when a second wave of enemy planes came in later that day we were able to shoot back. Perhaps not to much effect, but it was good for the soul. On 7 July 2005, I was a civilian with a family to look after—and all one could do was wait for what else might lie in store.

All this was happening quite quickly. Two uncomfortable thoughts lodged in my mind. From the information available it looked as though London was under attack from a series of comparatively small bombs mainly on the tube—but was the series complete after the bus bomb in Tavistock Square? Or worse, was the series of small bombs just a prelude to a 'spectacular' of some sort?

A year before I had taken part in a BBC Panorama programme in which a group of experts under the former Defence Secretary Michael Portillo tried to grapple with the effects of a terrorist attack on London. The communications expert was Lance Price who has recently published a book on his time in

Downing Street as Alastair Campbell's number two. I played the part of the cabinet office intelligence briefer, a task I had performed for real from 1999-2002.

We were organised as COBRA, the government's most senior crisis management committee. The atmospheric acronym (much loved by the producers of 'Spooks' and other spy-related dramas) stands for Cabinet Office Briefing Room A, the ultra-high tech underground command and communications centre beneath the Cabinet Office—shown off to President Putin on his recent visit to Downing Street. It is where our national response to an emergency or crisis is co-ordinated. A senior official or middle-ranking government minister is usually in the chair for more routine emergencies, with all the relevant departments and agencies represented as required, including the armed forces. In a serious crisis COBRA is chaired by the Foreign or Home Secretary and sometimes by the prime minister, as on 9/12 and indeed 7 July and 8 July. It is a very effective and professional way to make quick decisions in a crisis and a credit to both our political leaders and our civil service—who practise the procedures regularly.

The BBC's mock-up version was very much like the real thing. But, chillingly, in the scenario we played out a series of suicide tube bombs were just the prelude to a suicide detonation of a fully-laden chlorine tanker on Bishopsgate. In the exercise we were just about able to handle the tube bombs, but the chlorine tanker caused mass casualties and we were effectively overwhelmed.

Was something like this about to happen for real? I was like most Londoners that day afraid—partly of what had happened, but partly also of what more might happen during the day.

The mobile telephone network went down almost immediately, but I got through to home on the land-line. Used to giving orders in the army—it had been a relief to return to a more negotiated life-style—I was giving orders at this stage. Get everyone back home and then stay there. There must have been many calls like that on the day.

Luckily within minutes I knew where all the members of my family were. None of them travelled on the tube—I had long felt it was too dangerous, mainly because of the terrorist threat. The thought of frightened and bewildered children trapped under-ground had always haunted me. It was one of the minor blessings of both 9/11 (and 7 July it would turn out) that no children were killed. Natural claustro-phobia reinforced by my experiences in the Falklands meant that I rarely used the tube myself preferring a longer commute on the bus.

Everyone had been expecting some kind of attack on London—by Islamists. I had preached long and hard whenever I got the opportunity on television and in occasional articles in the press against the idea that terrorist attacks were inevitable—a corrosive doctrine that aggrandises terrorists and stokes fear and passivity into their intended victims.

I felt strongly (and still do) that we can so order our affairs to make terrorism of any kind very, very difficult to carry off—certainly much more difficult than on 7 July. But anyone with any knowledge of Islamist terrorism or London's vulnerabilities knew that someone was likely to have a crack at us at some point.

The telephone rang with a request to come to the Millbank television studios. I had been commenting for some time on the twin subjects of intelligence and terrorism—news and occasionally sustained analysis. There had been considerable spikes activity during the Hutton and later the Butler Inquiries on the intelligence role in the Iraq War.

Most of the leading UK and US channels had plans in place on how they would cover terrorist attacks in London and by a pre-arranged plan I made my way down on foot to Millbank studios opposite parliament to try and give some live 'expert' commentary and make sense of what had happened. When I left Russell Square the various channels we were monitoring were gradually piecing together events with emphasis naturally on what exactly had happened, how many casualties there had been, and who might have been responsible.

★ ★ ★

Millbank studios is an unusual place—all the major world networks have offices or hired space there, ranging from the big English-speaking channels to NHK—the Japanese equivalent of the BBC. Sitting in a TV studio less than two hours after the last bomb was an extraordinary and slightly strange experience.

I had heard one of the bombs go off and had walked down through the police cordon in Russell Square. I had experienced the effects of bombs in Northern Ireland and had survived a disastrous bombing in the Falklands. I knew about terrorism and had spent large parts of my 20s and 30s soldiering against the IRA. I knew about intelligence from my time in the Defence Intelligence Staff and the Cabinet Office. And I knew a bit about how the government would be trying to respond to the crisis having attended various COBRAs including the one on 9/12 chaired by Tony Blair. Latterly I had begun to know my way a little around television studios and understand how news bulletins are put together.

And here it all was in front of me—the media drama being played out. The real drama and tragedy had happened hours before but the interpretation we would put upon events was essentially still up for grabs.

I was irritated on arrival to see one of the foreign channels broadcasting a banner which read 'chaos and panic in London'. It was a rough day, particularly for those caught up in the bombs and their families—but there was absolutely no chaos and panic where I had come from, the scene pretty much of two of the bombs. Foreboding, fear, perhaps, but no panic and no chaos. Of course crisis management inevitably involves some improvisation—some of the lightly wounded were taken to hospitals by commandeered buses. But that just goes to show the professionalism and flexibility of emergency response staff. Sometimes one has to wonder about the media.

It was clear from the start that the rescue services and police and community support officers (unsung heroes often) on the ground had performed well. Anyone in London on that day could see that. Congratulations were in order for the rescue services and the passers by that helped, and the millions of calm resigned Londoners who just got on with their lives that day. Remember that they had no idea that the series of bombs had finished with the explosion on the Tavistock Square bus. In the past the IRA and other terrorist networks have used the tactic of the 'secondary device'. Set off a bomb causing death and injury. Wait until the emergency services have gathered and then set off another bomb designed to kill as many of them as possible.

I made a number of short appearances on various channels, and retired to a quiet corner to compose a newspaper article with a near impossible deadline and update myself through various contacts inside the studios and elsewhere.

I had an easy job—I knew and was finding out enough—to make informed comment which I hoped was helpful. And the TV professionals, graceful under pressure, haul you on and off when you are required, usually with some steer as to the latest angle but sometimes not—particularly with new and breaking facts. I remember saying on a number of occasions that the attacks so far, although horrible for those affected, were within London's resilience as a large city—or something on those lines. This was fair. It was becoming obvious as the day went on that this was not a catastrophic attack and the longer the delay in any follow-on attack, the safer we were becoming.

The great and the good were making their way into the studios. The Commissioner of the Metropolitan Police—shorter and less bulky than you would expect, and immaculate in his uniform—strode past, followed by what looked like a large staff. The poor man looked furious—as he should have been. Just before the bombs hit he had been doing a radio interview on how good the security was going to be for the 2012 Olympics. The leader of the opposition arrived, the movement of his legs obscured by desks and computer equipment, he seemed to glide across the floor.

It was widely accepted—though it may have remained unsaid for some time—that the bombs probably had an Islamist extremist origin. Some had been suggesting a North African connection and the word on the streets was that we were seeking help and advice from the Spanish authorities, which seemed to confirm this. Others, more ominously, were coming to the conclusion that these might be British plots. Everyone I spoke to that day was hoping that the perpetrators would not turn out to be British, but acknowledged the strong possibility that they might be.

As the day progressed, we were all probably right to be relieved. It was not 9/11. Yes it could have been worse if the attacks that had happened had been delivered in a different way. But once the initial facts of the attacks were established by the media doing their job to the best of their ability, a weirder atmosphere took hold—almost of self-congratulation.

Official spokesmen said over and over again that the situation was under control, over and over again how well the rescue services were doing, over and over again how well Londoners were facing up to the tragedy—as if somehow these things were separate from the realities on the ground and by saying them again and again we could make them true. I think in the end they were all true, but how did anyone know at the time?

And was it the right emphasis when so many of our fellow citizens had been horribly killed or wounded that day? Do not for a single moment believe that people die straight away in bombs. It may have been quick for some, but not for others. The message at the end of the day seemed to be almost like the administration of a public sedative.

★ ★ ★

My conclusion was rather different: I was furious like everybody else with the killers themselves. But I was also angry because it increasingly looked as if we had been caught off guard. It was a feeling confirmed when I discovered that the country's threat state had been reduced a few weeks before—without public announcement. How typical—an intelligence assessment system which did not appear to work (again) and that disseminates its information not on public channels but by a kind of 'old boy' network.

Common sense should have told us to be very much on our guard on 7 July. Although I had not been a particular supporter of the London Olympics bid— as I had sat on my bus early in the morning it had seemed a marvellous thing. Terrorists often seek out such moments to strike during major national events because they can achieve maximum publicity for their cause and inflict maximum propaganda damage on their enemies.

I felt strongly and still do that we had failed the people killed and wounded that day—badly. The way we were organising ourselves to protect our law-abiding citizens against the random and ghastly violence of terror had not worked.

There was also a strange sense of people pulling their punches. This is appropriate in these situations. Information is incomplete and the last thing anyone wants to do is cause panic or further distress on an already difficult day. Some of it could be explained by the strong sense on behalf of all commentators official and unofficial that the bombs should not be used to set one Briton against another.

If there had been riots or intimidation aimed at our Muslim communities and individuals in the aftermath we would have been playing directly into the hands of the terrorists themselves who seemed convinced that we are an intolerant people.

But also, and less laudably, on a day when official information was at a premium little nuggets of what looked like officially-derived or pronounced propaganda began to appear on all the news channels. The ground had been well prepared in advance with the endless Orwellian re-iteration that terrorist attacks were inevitable, but now the other two parts of the triad came into play—'the attacks came out of the blue' and 'everything which could have been done to prevent the bombings had been' .

The demands of 24-hour media coverage are great, but how did anyone know at that stage precisely how these bombings came about? And why were senior figures at pains to suggest that everything that could have been done to thwart the attacks had been done?

No one is suggesting that the government or anyone else did not truly believe they had done all they should to stop terrorist attacks. In the same way after an air-crash most would accept that the crew and the pilots of any given plane did all they could to keep the aircraft safe. But planes still go down often due to error. It is not a question of intentions but consequences.

The problem is that we are in danger of being warned off criticising crucial aspects of government behaviour. Ms Blears's (the number two at the Home Office and a very convincing, competent and thoughtful minister on matters of security) huffy and schoolmistressly put-down of suggestions that we should have a public inquiry is a good example. The thrust of the put-down was that at a time of high national threat ministers and the police and the security services have better things to do.

A cheap shot, it seemed to me—even on that day. We still need to know whether mistakes were made, and if so how. It is a matter of proper government in time of crisis.

The weirdness of it was that her put-down seemed not an attempt to shut down debate in panic before the press or public probed too deep into policy or operational mistakes, or started to ask the Iraq question. Ministers, security officials and others seemed to genuinely believe that the way they structured our intelligence and protective security is the best possible way.

Ministers and senior officials responded well to the human tragedy. Sympathy has its place and Mr Blair does it very well. It is a necessary part of government—we are so used to the Prime Minister emoting in the right way that we forget how necessary it is to have that capacity in the modern world. Look what happened when Mr Bush did and said the wrong thing as the tragedy of New Orleans was unfolding. We will miss this aspect of Mr Blair when he is gone in the same way that the Americans miss Mr Clinton.

This is not spinning—it is a proper function of a modern politician. But is that what we really pay them for? We pay their salaries—first and foremost to make sure that we are safe—not rich or even happy—but safe. Without safety nothing else will work and it will become increasingly difficult for us to remain prosperous. It is this less glamorous but more important function that is often underplayed.

Oddly, in a world where governments seem to do so much, they risk forgetting their core function.

* * *

And so the day drew to a close. Like everyone else I walked wearily home eventually hopping on a bus near the Albert Hall. The driver sweetly was not accepting any tickets. Jammed together on the bus people were less private and contained than usual—even the bearded Muslim guy next to me managed a weary half-smile as he was looked up and down for the umpteenth time.

Everyone was talking about the day's events. An American tourist said rather loudly to me 'Are you CIA—my father worked for them?' The smart embossed blue folder which I had been given on a visit to the CIA's headquarters in Langley, US, was clearly visible in my bag. The Muslim guy really was smiling now. In fact everyone thought it a huge joke. It was a good feeling on that double-decker bus—not the Blitz spirit, but a kind of resigned good humour. Very London.

Yet where was the official anger? Where were the flashes of aggression that we had seen in Messrs Giuliani and Bush after 9/11? All was not right with the world. We had been caught out but nobody seemed to accept that we could do better.

I thought then that somehow I should make my views known if possible—not in the television studios—expert commentary on terrorism and intelligence does not work that way—but in a piece of pungent analysis pinned on my experiences that day in both the real and the media world.

# The Rules of the Game

## *MI5, MI6 & others*

On 2 June the Joint Terrorism Analysis Centre (JTAC), which reports to the head of MI5 and is responsible for assessing the threat from international terrorism to the UK, lowered the national alert state from 'severe general' to 'substantial' with the words 'at present there is not a group with both the current intent and the capability to attack the UK'.

A confident prediction you would think, important enough for the JTAC to communicate to its 'customers'—the intelligence and security agencies of the United Kingdom and other institutions and private companies thought to be of importance to the national infrastructure and economy—but not to the general public.

JTAC's analysis was focussing on international terrorism and neither they, nor anyone else, would pretend that it had absolute analytical fidelity. But the prediction was a blunder nevertheless. As in a bad pantomime, the audience could have been shouting 'look behind you'.

Predicting terrorist attacks is a tricky business. But the disturbing thing about this assessment is that it was moving in diametrically the opposite direction to what was about to happen on the ground—and it was expressed with confidence.

Was it an intelligence failure? You bet.

The first question one needs to ask in this case is, could we have detected, disrupted or deterred the attacks?

Everyone else seemed to know that someone was about to have a go—except us. Like the cuckolded husband we had no idea until it actually happened in front of our eyes.

Both the French and the Saudis claim to have had assessments suggesting that we were about to be attacked. The French assessment (it is not clear whether it was ever passed to the British on liaison channels) predicted accurately that a plot would emerge from within radicalised elements of the Pakistani community in the UK. The Saudi information suggesting an attack in the UK had, according to its UK Ambassador Prince Turki al Faisal speaking on the Today Programme, been passed on in good time.

Early July 2005 was in any case a prime symbolic time to attack. It was not a crucial confluence of obscure dates in the extremist calendar apparent only to the die-hard Al Qaeda expert. It was staring us in the face—if we were looking.

The Gleneagles Summit had long been planned, Britain had just assumed the prestigious rotating presidency of the EU and London had been (unexpectedly) awarded the Olympic Games. Terrorists of all creeds try to choose the timing of their attacks very carefully—if they can. They like anniversaries, either of their own—the IRA were always active around Easter as a homage to and reminder of the Easter Rising against Britain in Dublin in 1916. Or they choose anniversaries important to their enemies—the IRA bombed the Remembrance Sunday Commemorations at Enniskillen in 1987. Terrorists also like to attack great public events which the whole world is watching in order to publicise their cause—as the PLO did at the Munich Olympics in 1972.

Sometimes the timing of an attack can be designed to catch an opponent off guard—the two most famous examples of this come from conventional war—the Japanese attacked Pearl Harbor on a Sunday on 7 December 1941, and Arab armies attacked Israel in October 1973 on the eve of Yom Kippur, the most solemn day in the Jewish religious calendar, when most soldiers would be at home with their families. The Israeli Defence Force still comes to a high state of alert before Yom Kippur—regardless of the intelligence picture. And this precautionary attitude has always pervaded the British Army whose units in the field invariably 'stand to arms'—every man in his fighting position with weapons ready—at dawn and dusk, the two most likely times of the day for an attack.

We should have been on some kind of precautionary alert in July. If the UK had been a military unit we would have doubled our sentries and 'stood to' at dawn—as a standard response. The question is why we weren't.

Instead we went to sleep, and even planned on siphoning London's policemen away from the capital.

A large number of Metropolitan policemen were deployed to assist with security at the Gleneagles summit. No doubt some trouble was expected in Scotland, but surely not terrorism—we know that MI5's JTAC had already assessed that no group had the capability or intention to attack the UK. London's missing policemen were taken from the capital not for anti-terrorist policing but to assist with civil order issues. (We were later told by the Metropolitan police commissioner that it made no difference and that the availability of these policemen would have had no effect on the level of policing in London in the run-up to the bombs.)

What of the attack itself?

We were not caught off guard by a high-grade super-fiendish Al Qaeda spectacular involving the sophisticated co-ordination of scores of agents and sympathisers across the globe accompanied by the unimaginable hijacking of several aircraft. This was a very standard plot hatched in Leeds—on our home turf—and led by a dangerous and plausible and British fanatic.

The attack appeared, like 9/11, to come 'out of the blue'. But (sadly) the situation is more complex than that. For the 7 July plot the trail centres around Siddique Khan, the presumed ringleader.

Clearly, he was a man of influence within his community. In his taped confession to murder aired two months later on Al-Jazeera, he came across as a typical finger-jabbing saloon-bar bore. It is possible that his disaffection was known or only suspected by a few in his community, although he appears to have been banned from the local mosque because he was a troublemaker.

Incredibly, for a plot that came out of the blue, the ringleader had come to the attention of the police previously. Not as part of an everyday police investigation, but as part of a major inquiry into an Islamist terrorist plot to blow up nightclubs in London, Operation Crevice. A highly successful and brilliantly executed counter-terrorist operation which saved many lives, Operation Crevice uncovered a sophisticated plot to use IRA-style home-made explosives in huge quantities to cause havoc and carnage across London's West End. Siddique Khan's name and possibly telephone number emerged during the investigations—apparently peripherally.

A look around Beeston and at Khan's passport might have produced a different result today. But the police and intelligence services have to prioritise and they did so during Operation Crevice. The authorities decided that he did not constitute a threat. The lead, like many others perhaps, was tragically not exploited.

The question in point is, would Siddique Khan have been able to plan and recruit for his attacks if he had remained on the surveillance radar? What was the backdrop of the decision not to follow up this lead further?

* * *

When examining intelligence failures one is usually not looking for stupidity or negligence, but for a form of 'groupthink'—a systematic flaw that creates a blind spot by making everyone think in the same way. Attention, or importance, or priority, is assigned to the intelligence that supports pre-existing views about enemy or terrorist behaviour.

Given that the central skill in counter-terrorist intelligence work is making connections between individuals however hard they try to disguise them— there must, for example, have been something about the profile of Siddique Khan that turned off the natural and often aggressive inquisitiveness of MI5 and Special Branch—despite the fact that his name had emerged out of an investigation into a potential Islamist extremist atrocity.

There may have been a simple bureaucratic reason—not enough MI5 agents or policemen to follow up every lead. All intelligence analysis takes place against both a formal background of 'requirements and priorities': jargon for what you think you need to know, how badly you need to know it, and the effort you are prepared to make to get the information. (But the members of the Security Service and special branch that I have worked with over the last twenty years nearly all shared a singlemindedness of purpose and restlessness of intellect that would lead them to consider again and again such intelligence wisps in the wind—even on their days off.)

Two other official factors may have played a part. First, Iraq. We know that MI5 accepts that the Iraq war has been a radicalising factor pushing a small number of British Muslims towards violence. But given the government's absolute unwillingness to accept a link between the British presence in Iraq and terrorism it would have been difficult for them expressly to give the correct priority to this question. Second, a lack of understanding or inquisitiveness on this matter would also tend to re-inforce (now old-fashioned) thinking about Islamist terrorism—that in the UK it is essentially an imported rather than home-grown or semi-home-grown phenomenon.

Further, there is a more informal, but equally powerful and pervasive 'atmosphere'—which includes both analytical suppositions, and sometimes a 'political charge'. This 'political charge' is not necessarily party-political, but a result of groups of officials being engaged in a great project: IRA disarmament, say, or war in Iraq.

It becomes very difficult in such an atmosphere to analyse critically any trends or events that run counter to any essential part of a risky government strategy, or any convictions which have embedded themselves in the minds of the most senior analysts.

That vital perquisite to sound analysis, the 'analyst's freehold', is easily compromised by poor organisation of atmosphere. Most successful intelligence assessment organisations are comprised of individuals with more or less equal status. There may be ranks and pay grades but the views of any analyst skilled enough to be selected for the group are respected. This is only common sense given that such groups are engaged in the most difficult task of all—looking into the future. When an analyst honestly dissents from the majority view or argues against a widely accepted assessment their position is never in question. They may be subjected to argument to modify their views but never pressure or what Lord Butler called in his report on intelligence and Iraq 'strain'.

Groupthink exists to an extent in any organisation, and it existed and exists within our intelligence and security services, too. The relevant question is therefore what it is, and whether such groupthink is actively encouraged, and whether it might have been a contributory factor in the run up to the bombings of 7 and 21 July, and so, crucially, whether it blunted both our analytical and operational capabilities and formed a serious threat to our security.

\* \* \*

Our current intelligence mindset appears to be based on an appeasing doctrine, the so-called 'Covenant of Security'. This refers to the long standing British habit of providing refuge and welfare to Islamist extremists on the unspoken assumption that if we give them a safe haven here they will not attack on these shores. French intelligence call this policy—with contempt— 'Londonistan'.

In addition to a physical Londonistan there would appear to be an analytical 'Londonistan'. The idea of the Covenant of Security pervades every aspect of our intelligence apparatus. It has champions both within official and academic circles, and nearly everything we do or plan for our security takes place within this doctrine.

If Londonistan really worked and its maintenance meant that there would never be attacks in the UK, there might be a more powerful case to be made for it. But the idea was always a mirage—predictably some of the extremist propaganda seems to have infected our own population. Harbouring sundry extremists in London was always selfish. 'I'm all right Jack' is hardly the way to go about increased European and world co-operation in the war on terror.

Yet the doctrine is still in rude health. The most recent example of this attitude was a leaked government memo—apparently from Mockbul Ali, the Foreign Office's Islamic Issues adviser.[1] It discusses dealing with the possibility of a visit to the UK by cleric Yusuf Al Qaradawi, who has been banned from visiting the US since 1999 for alleged terrorist links.

When he last visited London in 2004 the leader of the opposition Michael Howard demanded he be expelled. The Mayor of London Ken Livingstone compared him to Pope John XXIII and described him as 'the most powerfully progressive force for change and for engaging Islam with western values.'

You may or may not agree with either point of view—but what is interesting is the reason the memo gives for not banning the visit

> By taking such action the UK could turn mainstream Muslim opinion further against the UK and could encourage some to move to violence against British targets.

The shocking assumption in this quotation is that if the government can prove that a man is a sympathiser with terrorism and he is not allowed to visit the UK then mainstream Muslim opinion could turn against the UK.

British Muslims will shudder with disbelief about this extraordinary conclusion. We know that Islamist extremism is a powerful force currently in the world, but the idea that 'mainstream' Muslims identify with terrorism or are likely to be pushed towards terrorism because the UK refuses a visa to a controversial cleric seems bizarre. British Muslims roundly condemn the July attacks, yet they are treated by the government as if large numbers are forever on the verge of disloyalty to their native or adopted country and will erupt in violent rebellion.

To take an example from recent history which points up the absurdity of the claim—many Irishmen have sympathy with the idea of a united Ireland but that hardly made them supporters of the IRA's savagery, or likely to move towards supporting violence because the UK refused a visa to an IRA propagandist.

We never muddled our thinking or sensed that we could not take a stand over who we admit to this country in the case of the IRA. It is a healthy attitude that seems to have withered under the influence of the Covenant of Security in the case of Islamist terrorism.

★ ★ ★

There are other aspects of groupthink which complicate an adequate security response to 7 July.

We have been told that the security services had 'no specific intelligence' about the London attacks (how often have I heard this refrain before during my career). In effect, our intelligence services are saying—repeated by their political masters—we did not know because we did not know.

Is this an acceptable response one may well ask?

This is a tricky area and one in which people tend to betray their backgrounds. But it needs putting in context.

To the spy or collector of intelligence, say the equivalent of James Bond, the specific pieces of intelligence are of immense importance. Often gathered under conditions of danger or, in the case of signals intelligence, operating at the very edge of code-breaking or intercept technology, it assumes an importance and a status all of its own once dressed up with 'For Your Eyes Only' or some other suitably exclusive caveat. Slipped into a leather JIC folder and stamped with the words 'Approved by the Joint Intelligence Committee',* even the poorest and flimsiest pieces of 'intelligence' can end up seeming much weightier than they really are.

The most infamous example is the claim made in the 'dodgy dossier'[2] of September 2002 that 'military

* The Joint Intelligence Committee is the central body in the UK government's intelligence machinery. JIC members include the heads of the three security and intelligence agencies, the Chief of Defence Intelligence and sen-

planning allows for some of the Weapons of Mass Destruction to be ready within 45 minutes of an order to use them'. It was used to support the case for going to war in Iraq. In the words of the Prime Minister: 'It is unprecedented for the Government to publish this kind of document. ... I wanted to share with the British public the reasons why I believe this issue to be a current and serious threat.' Magnified in the press, this became the single most important plank in the case for going to war. Controversy still surrounds the claim which was based on a single source—that is to say a single person. Lord Butler later dismissed it in his inquiry suggesting that it should never have been included in the dossier or any other paper produced for the Joint Intelligence Committee.

It remains for all intelligence practitioners a stark warning of what can happen if too much weight is placed on a single piece of intelligence.

In other words, to the collector, the presence or absence of specific information is crucial to his view of threat, or of reality, and may loom larger in his mind than they should. But to the analyst such reports are just a part of the picture he (or she) is trying to build up. The individual pieces have much less status in his mind. He is more interested in the general overview and the likelihood of a threat surrounding it.

ior representatives of the Foreign & Commonwealth Office, the Ministry of Defence, the Department of Trade & Industry, the Home Office and HM Treasury.

The British system recognises this and makes the analysis of intelligence entirely separate from its collection.

Nonetheless, the collectors of intelligence (our James Bonds) believe that the world revolves around them. Analysts accept this in part, but tend to a more jaded view of the intelligence reality. In their view intelligence is only partly about analysing clandestine intelligence. An exaggerated respect for individual pieces of intelligence is not only inefficient but also skews the power relationship between the various parts of the intelligence community.

The job of the intelligence analyst is to make sense of the world and so secret intelligence is not all they use. The assessments staff in the cabinet office, for example, who actually write the papers for the JIC and prepare the intelligence briefings for Number 10 use secretly obtained intelligence as only a part of their analysis.

This is by design and followed on the common-sense conclusions of the Franks Report, which examined intelligence failures leading up to the Falklands War. In that report Franks warned against too much reliance on clandestine intelligence. Your highly placed sources at the heart of the Argentine navy may be telling you that there is nothing going on, but have a quick look at publicly available information such as activity in major docks or in the local newspapers and you will be more able to gauge the precise intentions of your enemy. Secret information is only a small part of the picture. There is so much you don't know that secret information should never be seen as presenting the whole picture.

Therefore, the nature of intelligence analysis is that, by definition, you don't know the precise nature, extent, or detail of a threat. If you did, you would of course be in a good position to stop it.

To expect this level of knowledge for each terrorist plan that is hatched is to miss the point. It postulates a state of mind and level of expectation that is impossible to satisfy (and by extension an easy excuse when things go wrong). The chances that you will gather specific knowledge on a specific attack are low unless you have physically or electronically penetrated the cell that is about to carry it out. One has to accept that it is a given in many instances that you will not know who specifically is going to do what, when, so that you may arrest or stop them.

But what you can always do is to arrange your security measures in such a way as to make those attacks extremely difficult or at least more difficult to carry out. We do this up to a point by assessing both the 'threat' and issuing 'alert' levels.

As mentioned, threat assessment* is the responsibility of MI5's Joint Terrorism Analysis Centre (JTAC), and it attempts to gauge the intentions and capability

---

* JTAC currently uses a moving scale in descending order: Level One—Critical; Level Two—Severe General; Level Three—Substantial.

of any terrorist group. What would these terrorists like to do, or what are they planning to do, and the extent to which they can carry it off. Intention and capability do not necessarily match up well. The most murderous and ambitious terrorist group may not pose a high threat if, say, they cannot put together a bomb competently.

'Alert' levels are not set by JTAC but are the responsibility of 'local planners'—the Ministry of Defence for instance sets its own alert state. The levels dictate the effort and resources which are put into guarding the government estate (ministries, army barracks) and critical national infrastructure (transport networks, power stations, parts of the City of London). And, in the words of Home Secretary Charles Clarke,

> While the alert state is heavily influenced by the threat level, it is JTAC which sets the threat level independently and is not responsible for deciding on what mitigating action should be employed. Hence the reduction in threat level was not directly connected to the alert state and was for local planners to determine. There was therefore no significant diminution to specific protective measures.[3]

But, whatever the intricacies of the connection between the 'threat' and 'alert' levels, and the precise difference between 'severe general' and 'substantial', it is almost impossible to defend that there was no 'significant diminution to specific protective measures'.

The authorities felt comfortable enough about the prospects of a terrorist attack on the UK not to brief the public on the threat and to despatch policemen from London and other parts of the country in large numbers to protect the G8 Conference at Gleneagles from public order difficulties. Moreover, after the attack they had to be hurried back to the capital where they were needed. Whichever way you turn it, the system failed—fatally. We were but fortunate that the attack was relatively small.

Putting aside the question of whether Siddique Khan's peripheral connection to the March 2004 bomb plot discovered as part of Operation Crevice could have been turned into specific intelligence, the error in this case appears to stem from a misappreciation of the extent to which the aims and aspirations of international terrorists have penetrated into small elements of the UK's domestic Muslim population. It is fair to conclude from the plotters' trips to Pakistan that there may also be an international connection, as yet undiscovered.

The failure is not that MI5's JTAC did not pick up knowledge of this plot (very difficult), but that it failed to give us the correct background picture against which our intelligence and security assets should have been operating (a much less daunting task).

We may never know because the details of intelligence assessments of this sort are rightly kept secret. But it looks as though JTAC placed too much importance on specific intelligence—namely its absence. At any rate, that is how Home Secretary Charles Clarke defended JTAC's lowering of the threat level—'a judgement on the available intelligence'.[4]

This unwillingness to look beyond the specific intelligence, seems to be a straightforward retreat to the errors that led to the Franks Inquiry.

★ ★ ★

Throughout our analysis of the intelligence events of 7 July two factors re-appear.

The first factor is bureaucratic friction—was all the proper information passed on in a timely fashion (and why is specific intelligence given such importance)?

Other friendly nations—France and Saudi Arabia had assessments which suggested strongly that there would be an attack on the UK at the time. The Saudi assessment—which may have been based on specific intelligence—was certainly passed on to us. But we do not know what happened to it. The usual channel for such a report would be for it to be handed over to the officer in MI6 with responsibility for liaising with the Saudi intelligence services. He would make an initial assessment of its reliability and then pass it on to MI5's JTAC. We do not know if the French passed their assessment on through liaison channels. The Home Secretary has suggested that foreign liaison was an area he was going to have a close look at.[5]

The events of the day are also suffused with a conflation of what is home and what is overseas. Britons of emigrant descent murder other Britons in the UK using techniques invented overseas, and appear at least in part motivated by what the British are doing overseas. In other words, it is clear that in the most up-to-date version of Islamist extremist terrorism there is no distinction between home and overseas.

And yet we have two separate intelligence services whose responsibilities are split precisely along these old-fashioned lines. Worse, the long-standing strain of this split is well-documented and is so commonly known that it is standard lore of spy thrillers. It is, moreover, a split that is officially sealed by different terms of service. SIS or MI6 agents (the James Bonds) are part of the diplomatic service with all the perks and status that attach to that lofty department. Security Service or MI5 personnel are usually employed on less lucrative Home Civil Service terms.

The London plots, however, show clearly that there is no real-world division of responsibility. When it comes to Islamist terrorism there is no home and there is no abroad—just a continuum.

In a sense what happens on the sub-continent is as much a subject for the Security Service as it used to be when security there was a matter for MI5 before

1947. Security Service agents require experience in South Asia as much as Beeston. And the reverse is true for MI6. There is no longer a point that is served by the distinction between the services.

Is it really possible to gather counter-terrorist intelligence in Islamabad or elsewhere if you do not have a proper understanding of the bread and butter of tracking down terrorism in Ilkely? From the start our intelligence officers, even as new recruits, are not taught to operate in global terms—and their lifetime network of professional contacts are limited by their location in one or other organisation. Everything our intelligence officers do is based on this division of responsibility—home equals MI5, abroad equals MI6.

It used to create difficulties and tensions in Northern Ireland, too. Legally Northern Ireland and the Republic of Ireland are separate entities—of course. But in intelligence gathering terms North and South essentially formed a single unit with what happened on the UK mainland as a separate issue. Liaison and consultation between the two services may have worked well enough for Irish terrorism twenty years ago, but then the IRA was split along the same lines as the intelligence services—a part that dealt with home (all Ireland) and abroad (usually this meant the UK mainland but latterly Europe as well).

Islamist terrorists recognise no such division of responsibility. It is time to consider this reality against the question whether an intelligence system that thought globally would have performed better in run up to 7 July.

Most advanced countries still operate a system like ours—responsibilities for human intelligence split into home and abroad—but it is instructive to see that the eavesdroppers in both the UK and the United States belong to a single national signals intelligence service with global responsibilities.

It is also worth looking at what the United States has done in the aftermath of 9/11—an attack in which many US citizens died but which was planned abroad and carried out by foreigners, some with residency. The US is of course a much bigger place than the UK and the federal bureaucracy is difficult to reform efficiently. Congressional control of the purse strings and the need to pass laws to change federal institutions make it complicated for President Bush to impose his reforming will.

Yet the US has managed to streamline its intelligence organisations—because it had to. Two separate bureaucracies still exist under separate control—the Federal Bureau of Investigation for home matters and the Central Intelligence Agency for abroad (and numerous other agencies of various types). But they report to a new Director of National Intelligence—John Negroponte, significantly previously US Ambassador to Iraq. He has the exclusive ear of the president on intelligence matters—replacing the Director of the CIA in this role, whose status has been reduced. Negroponte's job is to implement The Intelligence Reform and Terrorism Prevention Act of 2004 (the two subjects are closely and formally linked in the American mind). The Act gives the force of law to improving liaison and analysis in the US intelligence organisations' effort and brings them all under the day to day control of a single man.

The second factor that crops up is undue political influence on the intelligence apparatus. During the run-up to the Iraq war it is clear and widely accepted (cf Lord Butler's report) that analysts and collectors came under intense pressure to produce intelligence. So much pressure in fact that the suspicion remains that some of it was made up: the 45 minutes discussed above was subsequently withdrawn by MI6—an almost unheard of measure for such a crucial piece of intelligence. The Joint Intelligence Committee, supposedly independent of government (like JTAC), appeared to have actually been run by Downing Street officials for a time—though these allegations were never confirmed. In other words at a time of crisis, when hard facts are most in demand, the most senior (and illustrious) intelligence analytical body in the country buckled under political pressure.

What kind of pressure, one may well ask, for example, was at work on the JTAC when it lowered, for example, its threat level on 2 June?

★ ★ ★

In one sense we have been here before. The controversies surrounding the setting of the UK's interest rates in the early 1990s—the feeling that they were being manipulated for political advantage rather than economic stability—gave rise on Gordon Brown's first day in office as chancellor to the independence of the Bank of England from government interference in this matter. Our interest rates are now set independently by a committee of experts who meet at the Bank of England each month. They have to take into account a number of technical requirements laid down by the government, most importantly an inflation target. The Bank of England has its own agents who gather large quantities of market intelligence from individuals, businesses and shopping centres around the country. The Committee also has to take into account economic conditions across the world and how they might impact on the UK. And they have to make an assessment on what to do with the interest rate. Widely people accept this as fair and sensible as the country's best shot at getting it right—because the assessment is produced independently.

The process the committee goes through sounds remarkably similar to that of intelligence assessment. If interest rates must be kept away from political manipulation by the creation of a new institution, the same must surely be true of how we go about collating and assessing the threat to us all from terrorism.

The prime minister's pre-holiday statement was

45

that 'the rules of the game have changed'. He was right. And we must change how we play the intelligence game against Islamist extremists—it is 'the Great Game' of the early 21st century. We have to question our antiquated divided intelligence structure. Aimed at protecting a distant early 20th-century Empire, it does not trace the blue-print of the modern terrorist, gives rise to narrow views, and, worst, opens the door wide to undue political interference where independence is required.

# 3

# The Aftermath

*Security Forces*

Were top security officials in a state of panic after 7 July? Was their official response collected and decisive? Was the full measure of a well-honed and professional security force brought to bear on preventing repeat attacks in the wake of the tragedy?

We were assured by the Metropolitan police commissioner Sir Ian Blair that it had made no difference that policemen had been sent up to Scotland before 7 July, and that the availability of these policemen would have had no effect on the level of policing in London in the run up to the bombs.

It seemed a bold statement to make as in the aftermath of the 7 July bombs the principal tactic of the police was to flood the streets with armed police and additional plain clothed police were deployed to mingle into crowds and keep an eye on the situation in high risk areas such as the tube.

As we have seen, when the government raises threat levels and increases vigilance, it is a way of making it tougher for terrorist cells to execute their plans. In the face of visibly toughened security terrorists, even suicide terrorists, begin to lose confidence and become nervous. They cannot be sure that the authorities have not got an inkling of their plot. Every bag or identity check means possible discovery or the attack not being pressed home as planned. Every armed policeman or member of the public who looks twice at them with suspicion becomes a threat.

Indeed policemen at ports and airports are often armed with automatic weapons not because they are expecting a large-scale shoot out but as a deterrent. The terrorist knows that the hail of bullets shuts the door on escaping if his plans are aborted. During the first Gulf War I lived with my soldiers at Heathrow for nearly a week as part of a security operation there. The specialised policemen who look after airports were more than capable of handling the security but the deployment of armed troops was felt to be a deterrent to potential terrorists and re-assuring to the public. The public very openly welcomed our presence and we must have looked fairly frightening to anyone intent on mischief. Had something happened, the support offered would have been highly efficient.

As a preventive deployment, this kind of security

works well. But, after the fact, it may have the opposite effect and can look like desperation—a spray gun rather than a swat team. Instead of demonstrating a command of the situation, terrorist cells may scent panic, particularly if opening boxes of newly-minted policemen are seemingly the only strategy one has.

What else did security officials do in the aftermath of July 7?

In the months after 7 July there was little sense that Scotland Yard had intelligence on the new domestic Al Qaeda inspired threat. As on 7 July, they seemed to be writing on a big blank canvas, asking the public at large to help out. This is the 'Crimestoppers' approach to Islamist terrorism. It has its place, one supposes, but it is hardly re-assuring for the British population to realise that telephone calls to the police will not just be helping the police with their inquiries—they may be all the police have to go on. Is this really all that one can think of with millions of pounds spent on the prevention of terrorism?

Panic at the top often seeps down the hierarchy. Responsibilities, which should be clear-cut, start overlapping, and the further down the chain the more these responsibilities leave room for internal conflict or confusion. The uncertainty at the top becomes contagious at the bottom. What should be clearly expressed orders become unfocused or open to varying interpretation. Fatigue and stress can lead to confusion. Time pressures can lead to the taking of short-cuts and the disregarding of laid-down procedures.

It is one of the reasons why the armed forces—who typically operate in an atmosphere of maximum chaos and maximum fatigue—are trained right from the very start to issue and obey clear orders. Orders must always be comprehensive enough for a soldier to know what he is expected to do—even if he is cut off from or loses communications with his commanders.

The unfortunate killing of Mr de Menezes is both a tragic and instructive episode for an accurate impression of the rehearsedness of top level police command and control. Maybe the atmosphere of the high command was one of calm deliberation rather than drama. It is hard to know the answer from the outside. But actions and consequences are telling in these situations.

Possibly only terrorists themselves have a problem with the use of lethal force—at whatever stage of their mission they are identified—against suicide bombers. The question is not so much, should we kill them to avoid bloodshed? Rather, the issue is—how can we make sure they are suicide bombers before we act? Unlike a war situation the terrorists are not wearing the other side's uniform (and the presumption is that you were probably right to kill) but are the enemy within. We may therefore demand that procedures are designed with exacting rationality, particularly given the amount resources spent on them. There may be a war on terror, but none of us wants to be held ransom to fortune by being in the wrong place at the wrong time when decisions to kill are made by our security forces.

The police high command, often the most visible during national crisis, may have received no adequate or timely intelligence briefing or support from other parts of the nation's security apparatus in the weeks after 7 July. This looks fairly likely. Intelligence had little to offer and the police found themselves as both the first and last line of defence against an unknown number of further attacks. The 21 July plotters showed clearly on the day of the de Menezes killing that the attacks earlier that month could not be dismissed as a one off. It must have been an extremely stressful period for police commanders let alone the bobby on the beat. And crucially, by 21 July the police by Sir Ian Blair's own admission, were tired.

When the news began to come in of the shooting, my pulse quickened—to shoot dead a suicide bomber (whatever the precise circumstances) without other casualties was a great achievement for the security forces. When Sir Ian Blair confirmed that the shooting was connected with the previous day's events, I must admit I was even excited. All the training of the police, all the rehearsal of different scenarios had paid off—even under the difficult conditions the police were operating. When the descriptions of the individual who had been shot began to come out—bulky coat, vaulted the ticket barrier, refused to obey a police challenge—it seemed certain that he had been a suicide bomber.

It was a shock to discover over the following days that descriptions circulating in the media, and supposedly from official sources describing Mr de Menezes's appearance and behaviour, were untrue. Events became all the more mysterious when it emerged that members of the surveillance team following de Menezes had been sitting close to him—were they happy to do this because they could see that he could not be carrying a bomb?

Troublingly, the media and the public had been led to believe a state of events that was not just wrong, but was known to be unfounded. Officials, including Sir Ian Blair, must have known this on the day—either from public witnesses of the killing or from the operatives themselves—or very shortly after. It is challenging if not impossible to see the rationale for the smoke screen, and even harder to imagine that such a response was in the rule book carefully prepared for handling with sensitive errors such as the one that happened.

It is tempting to read in these events that particular people or departments acted incompetently. There may or may not be instances of this: the individual responsibilities of the day are the subject of a detailed official investigation being conducted—out of the public eye. But this is irrelevant for an assessment of the response of the security services as a whole.

We know that members of a police firearms unit shot eleven bullets at close range (three missed) while restraining and pushing Mr de Menezes to the ground. If he had been a suicide bomber the three agents would now be celebrated as heroes. But we know that Mr de Menezes, a Catholic, was nothing of the kind. On the admission of the police, he did not behave, look, or was previously suspected of being an extremist. Yet somehow, after having being tagged by mistake as a potential terrorist, the fatal mistake seems to have stuck.

One troubling aspect is therefore how the information disqualifying Mr de Menezes did not reach the person with authority to cancel the order to kill given under Operation Kratos (the code name for the procedures under which suspected suicide bombers can be killed).

Two points may be made. Interestingly, in a counter-terrorist situation the army cannot issue orders to kill. The individual soldier must make up his mind within a small set of 'rules of engagement'—usually printed on a small card—whether he is justified in killing. Further, consider the fact that—certainly since 9/11—plans to deal with an attack on the tube have been given detailed consideration in various scenarios. We have known for at least 4 years that security forces need to be able to communicate in the tube. Indeed one of the operational difficulties identified by the distinguished police and rescue experts I worked with on the Panorama programme referred to earlier was that it was very difficult for them to communicate underground. The police knew this as they also knew that the tube was a likely target for suicide bombings. Yet, there is nothing to suggest that Operation Kratos seems to have taken this into account.

★ ★ ★

What should we conclude on the basis of the facts we know?

One can read the tragedy of 22 July bluntly as a reason to end the shoot to kill policy under Operation Kratos.

Regional forces, for example, are less keen and have used tasers (electronic stunguns) in the counter-terrorist role effectively. When dealing with a suicide bomber about to go off in a crowded place, it is likely that the bomber in question has to press a button to detonate his bomb. You need to kill him so convincingly and quickly so that no twitching in his body could possibly depress the switch (this is the reason behind what looked like overkill at Stockwell tube station). But in principle a taser works as effectively.[6]

Abandoning the policy will, however, reduce the overall pressure that weighs on a suicide bomber as he carries out his intentions. We rely on the stress surrounding suicide bombers contributing to them making mistakes and reducing their lethality. Experience in the Middle-East teaches us that suicide bombers sometimes strike with little effect because the attacker mis-times or otherwise bungles the operation—through stress or fear of detection. The bomb on the Number 30 bus in Tavistock Square would almost certainly have killed more people if the bomber had been in a cooler possession of his faculties. The pressure that lethal force provides is an essential tool in our anti-terrorist armoury. It makes the delivery of suicide bombs to targets more difficult if any suicide bomber on his way to commit murder has the thought at the back of his mind that at any moment the person sitting next to him may turn around and kill him.

But when a whole system shows signs of shock and fatigue in the face of what were at the end of two weeks quite small terrorist attacks, it suggests that certain basic assumptions have been broken. The unimaginable has happened. It seems likely that the fact that the plot was hatched by two groups of British Muslims living in the UK rather than by foreigners had implications for policing that had been lost sight of under the Covenant of Security.

Whatever the case may have been, the official response in the aftermath of 7 July was as insufficient as that of the intelligence services before the tragedy. The organisation at the front line seem to have been hampered from within and from the top to respond publicly with the accuracy, foresight and decisiveness that one has come to expect. Like the structure of our intelligence services this demands thorough investigation as happened in the US after 9/11 and in Spain after the Madrid bombs. This is the pregnant question that calls for further investigation.

We had four years to prepare for these attacks—can we really maintain that we performed well enough?

# 4

# Thursday 21 July

## Borders

*Is it really possible that no one beyond the bombers had any inkling of their intentions? Were their extremist views and plans unknown even in the circle of friends and fellow Muslims who may have shared their fanaticism and hostility to the society in which they grew up.*

*The Times*—Leader 9 July 2005

This time I got the call before the news began to break publicly.

The television networks were very quick off the mark. And the day was very different—everyone who went into work on 21 July, however hassled and fatigued and frightened, eventually made it home that evening—though we did not know it at the time. The news of more bombs produced a strong feeling of dread—regardless of how serious they had been, it meant that the bombs on 7 July had not been a one off. Even more disturbing as the news began to come in it appeared that the attacks were trying to mimic those of two weeks before.

None of the possible scenarios looked re-assuring.

Either the plots were similar because they were linked—in some way suggesting a well-organised Islamist terror network able to strike more or less at will. Or the 21 July plotters were 'copy cats'—unconnected to 7 July but doing their bit for the cause by mimicking their more successful predecessors—which suggested that there might be an almost limitless supply of similar Islamist gangs dotted around the country. The second option was the one that really worried me, and may well turn out to be closer to the truth of what happened.

But it was clear from the start the bombs had not detonated properly. It may be that the bombs were designed to harass rather than kill—although the police doubt this. Whatever the facts turn out to be, the scenario felt like the kind of thing the IRA used to do in the 1980s—blow up a few railway lines in order to make everyone's commute a total nightmare.

London ground to a halt again, and this time round I found myself in the open air on a police cordon near the University College Hospital where a number of camera crews had gathered. You could feel the tension relax among the police (and the rest of us) as it slowly became clear that London had escaped a second day of carnage.

* * *

Nonetheless, this day had its own specific problems. Hussain Osman, one of the alleged 21 July bombers— the object of one of the biggest manhunts in British history—was able to escape from the country a few days later on the Eurostar after walking past his own wanted poster in Waterloo Station. He was not whisked away from a remote spot on the Norfolk coast by Al Qaeda, or shook off pursuers because— like Conan Doyle's Moriarty—he was a master of disguise. The legitimate question may be asked how he was able to walk calmly through Waterloo station and its extensive security checks. We are still waiting for the facts that explain how Hussain Osman was able to slip the net with such spectacular success.

Borders are difficult in the modern world. Before the EEC became the EU, crossing our borders could be difficult. The queues to cross the border points between France and Italy in the 60s, for example, could be horrendous. Now we can travel from one end of the continent to another without having to show any identity papers—either at national borders or, often, in hotels.

The movement of people is usually presented positively. Clearly these developments have had both economic and convenience benefits that we have got used to. But in the present circumstances they have a security downside. They make it very difficult to gather intelligence on likely terrorist suspects and much easier for terrorists to move around with impunity. We only have to ask ourselves the question whether abandoning control of our borders made terrorist attacks more or less likely?

We now have according some estimates a million illegal immigrants. The vast majority are here to better themselves and their families, no doubt, and are law-abiding, except for their illegal residence in this country. But we do not know enough about any of them. Their presence suggests an unofficial parallel world which may be economically vibrant and necessary, but which also provides an ideal recruiting ground for radicals from abroad.

★ ★ ★

The Home Secretary Charles Clarke in one of his public pronouncements in the aftermath of the bombings suggested that tracking down terrorists was like looking for a needle in a haystack.

We seemed to accept this without demur, but is Mr Clarke's sweeping statement true?

Tracking down small, tightly knit groups of supporters in the aftermath of a bomb plot is difficult where the principal actors have killed themselves in the attacks. But is the same really true where the plot failed and images of the perpetrators are available—specific intelligence if you wish?

Some consider certain animal activist organisations terrorist groups. Their belief—a passion for animals—is probably shared by the large majority of the British population. A haystack indeed. But IRA terrorists were (are?) by definition Catholic Irishmen (with may be one or two exceptions)—however much those of Catholic Irish descent may have wished the IRA did not claim to kill on their behalf, and may have suffered under the ruthless intimidation practised by the IRA. Were they 'a haystack'? Over the past thirty years there would have been as little point in contemplating an IRA plot coming from the thriving Muslim population in, say, Beeston as there would have been from within a protestant community in Belfast. We knew where to look for the IRA.

The same is true of Islamist terrorism. We now know for a fact that terrorist attacks on Britain may be undertaken by radical British Muslims who believe in violence rather than democratic protest. These are doubtless trying times for the British Muslim community, as their religious identity is being misappropriated by splinter groups claiming to act under their banner. But it is hard to imagine that any British Muslim would disagree that greater transparency of their community is needed to prevent further attacks. It is clear both that they roundly condemn the July attack and that they welcome further measures.

In a sense all counter-terrorist work is local—this is especially true of home-grown terrorism. Know your enemy remains the first commandment of intelligence operations and analysis. It has, for example, become apparent that all is not quite as it seems or as it should be in Beeston, the home ground of three of the four 7 July plotters. There were late-night meetings attended only by fellow fanatics, and there are social workers who are only willing to speak on condition of anonymity.

We need Muslim help with new security procedures. First with the vexed subject of profiling— always a sensitive issue in a multi-cultural society. The police do not currently stop and search on the basis of profiling. If you can only stop and search a limited number of people who should you target— Presbyterian South Sea Islanders or young Muslim men? Just as Irishmen knew perfectly well that they were likely to be stopped and questioned in an effort to prevent an IRA outrage, so do Muslims understand the situation now. It is something that has to be properly handled as those looking for offence will doubtlessly find and foment it.

Second, we need the help of Muslim leaders in formulating new surveillance and deportation rules.

Consider what the Home Secretary told the House of Commons Home Affairs Committee:

We have hundreds of people under surveillance.[7]

No doubt he was paying a compliment to the efforts of the Security Service and police (and we are led to understand military surveillance experts as well).

We shall never know the precise conditions surrounding the mounting of all this surveillance, but is it really necessary? Is it the right application of public money? Are all the subjects of the surveillance British citizens for instance? In the case of the IRA, non-British members were either not given permission to enter the country or were deported. If any of the current people under surveillance are not British, it would be simpler, safer and more sensible to deport them forthwith if they are of sufficient interest in terms of Islamist extremism to be under 24-hour surveillance.

Third, as well as improving our security we need to improve our understanding of British terrorism. We need a proper taxonomy of terrorism and its motives. The official position would currently appear to be: they are mad fanatics—everyone who sympathises with their aims in any way (including bringing about a western withdrawal from the Middle East) is also a mad fanatic.

But the IRA are not mad fanatics—which is why we have allowed two serving members of the IRA to become ministers in the Northern Ireland government. Some of them probably are mad fanatics but pretending that everyone who disapproves of our military intervention in the Middle East is a mad fanatic is running away from reality.

# 5

## The French Do It Better

### Intelligence

The Italians returned Hussain Osman, the suspected July 21 tube bomber, to the UK within two months of the UK applying for his extradition. This happened despite a vigorous and glamorous legal defence played out in the world media.

In contrast, Rachid Ramda, who is wanted by the French police in connection with the bombing of the Paris Metro in 1995, has spent 10 years in the English courts trying to avoid extradition to Paris.

One begins to understand the French undertone of contempt when they use the word 'Londonistan'. Our border security is so poor that Osman, the most wanted man in modern British history, was able to abscond to Italy under the noses of a massive police and intelligence operation. Yet even after 10 years we are unable to extradite a suspected bomber into the arms of the French judicial system.

★ ★ ★

We generally rely on our experience in Northern
Ireland as a source or cause of our skill in dealing with
terrorism. The modern British Army owes many of its
impressive skills to the leadership qualities and practical techniques previously required for soldiering in
the Province. Some of the best tools available in the
fight against terror were forged in Northern Ireland.
14 Intelligence and Security Coy (now The Special
Reconnaissance Regiment) of the UK Special Forces
Group are widely agreed to be the best surveillance
specialists in the world. Rumoured to have been lent
to the Colombian Government to help out against the
FARC and to Prime Minister Aznar to help Spain's
fight against ETA, the regiment is recruited from all
three services and they are a formidable group of people.

Along with other Ulster-derived security and
intelligence elements, these assets are now available in
the fight against Islamist terrorism on the UK mainland. In fact there is nothing unusual in this—intelligence and surveillance assets from across the spectrum
have previously been used on mainland UK when
appropriate—particularly in the physical monitoring
of IRA sympathisers in London in the 1980s and possibly further afield. The most formidable weapon

against terrorism to have emerged from our long struggle against the IRA was probably the Special Branch of the Royal Ulster Constabulary—now effectively disbanded and its confidential records compromised as result of the Good Friday Agreement.

Our security record in Ireland, at least after the early days, was admirable and by the mid 1980s we had a reasonable grasp often of when the IRA would try to strike on the mainland and a good feel for the background intelligence atmospherics.

As a result we feel somehow confident that we are 'good at dealing with terrorism'. To an extent that is true. But Ireland may have made us complacent in our attitude towards new types of terrorism. Because of the peculiar social and historical conditions in the Province it may have made us susceptible to the kind of arrangements of the Covenant of Security, or 'Londonistan'.

In Northern Ireland we were only trying to keep the lid on terrorism—the authorities never made any strong efforts to extinguish either the IRA or the various equally unpleasant protestant gangs. It would have been difficult in the extreme to shut down the IRA— they enjoyed (then) more or less secure bases in the south and a ready and lavish supply of funds from sympathisers in the United States with a pre-9/11 attitude to terrorism in other people's countries.

We allowed ghettoes to emerge which were under the effective control of terrorist organisations of one sort or another who operated as gangsters in their own communities. Provided things did not get out of hand, there was a live-and-let-live policy. The ghettoes and the violence are more or less still in place in both communities years after the Good Friday Agreement. The brutal murder of Robert McCartney in a Belfast bar in January 2005 highlights the point. A lifelong supporter of Sinn Fein from a hardline Republican enclave in north Belfast—he was beaten and butchered by IRA men after a minor altercation with one of them. There were numerous witnesses none of whom came forward to help the police. Grotesquely the IRA offered to shoot the men who had been responsible. And so on.

Maybe this was a reasonable price to pay for a kind of 'peace' in Northern Ireland, but we should beware of taking too much pride in our security achievements there. Our experience in the Province only goes so far. The Irish precursor of the 'Covenant of Security' is hardly possible with Islamist extremists. The security implications of hardline Muslim ghettoes under the intimidatory control of Islamist extremists are too alarming to contemplate.

Yet this is what the Covenant of Security opened the door to. The extremists we allowed into our country seem to have infected our own people with distrust of our democratic government. We need to look at how our native Muslim areas actually work. Who are the opinion-formers in such communities?

Perhaps we will find arrogance and intimidation by a small number. Crucially this arrogance and intimidation, despite the best efforts of sensible men and women, has been allowed to flourish for far too long and we have ourselves to blame.

We have allowed the process of knowing our enemy to become too exotic. There may be a mystery in the initial gestation of the individual suicide bomber (although this too is often overstated). Suicide or near-certain-death operations are common enough even in modern Western armies. But the mechanics of how they spread their dangerous message will no doubt turn out to be familiar enough.

There is an uncomfortable parallel with Northern Ireland. We never expected the people of the nationalist areas to be loyal to Queen and country—the whole point at issue was that Northern Ireland had never felt much affection for Britain. The day the Galahad was bombed during the Falklands War some of the people in nationalist West Belfast celebrated openly in the streets and taunted the British soldiers on patrol there—who would rather have been fighting in the Falklands. The nationalist Irish have a traditional grudge against the British. In their view we stole their land and allowed them even in modern times to be discriminated against by a government with the backing of Westminster.

But the history of Muslim communities in Britain is much more pragmatic as a place of immigration where their families have established successful lives. Yet through, for example, the extremists being freely given access to our country under the Covenant of Security we created our own jeopardy. The tragedy is that what took hundreds of years of resentment and mismanagement to create in Ireland, we have allowed to take hold in our Muslim communities in less than a generation. It is too easy to preach religious extremism in this country. Yet have we done enough to support moderates? Our studied neglect has empowered those who do not deserve respect, and eroded the esteem for those who do.

★ ★ ★

The rules of the game have changed and we need new techniques to fight a new threat. On arrival in the Cabinet Office new recruits are reminded of the great intelligence blunders of the past and what can be done to avoid repeating the mistakes in the future. The Covenant of Security may well be one of those.

Rather than look to our past dealings with the IRA to plan for the future, we should look abroad for inspiration, and France should be at the top of our list. For nearly a quarter of a century I have assisted in the fighting of terrorism in Northern Ireland and analysing intelligence in London and elsewhere, and during that time I have found no equal to French intelligence assessments and news gathering.

French society works in a different way from our own. There are all kinds of reasons from history why the French thwart and control home-grown terrorism better than we do. The most important one is that since the time of the Revolution in 1789, if not before, French leaders need to know what is going on in Paris. They need to take the pulse of Paris, otherwise they could be out of a job—a head in earlier times. Not too long ago the French state faced two crises which nearly brought it down—the terrorist campaign and political instability associated with the withdrawal from Algeria and the student troubles surrounding the events of 1968. The nearest British equivalent goes back to Guy Fawkes and it is difficult for us to grasp the violent undercurrent of turmoil in France that has such force.

The French are also in a weaker position than Britain. They have a much bigger native Muslim population, a large section of which has vivid memories of French withdrawal from Algeria and the savage war the French fought to keep hold of their North African colonies. It all happened as recently as forty years ago and there are plenty of people who can recall precisely the emotions of the time. Crucially, France is not an island—French borders are much more difficult to control and the influx of North African illegal immigrants in particular difficult to stem.

As they have a much longer experience with home-grown extremism, there is much to commend their tough attitude to their own national security. It is an important practical consideration which their politicians take seriously, and which their legal and police systems are designed to support.

It is hard to imagine a group of Islamist extremists threatened with deportation taunting M Sarkozy the current French Interior Minister on television the way Mr Clarke has been taunted by some and their legal advisers in the UK. Sheikh Omar Bakri Mohammed's provocative appearances on television and the radio on 21 July discussing amongst other things deportation and British foreign policy would simply not have been possible in France. He is of course now holidaying in Lebanon. The French Interior Minister is respected not because of the personality of any temporary incumbent (although M Sarkozy has proved especial-ly vigorous) but because he is powerful. In France you upset the police and intelligence services at your peril. And if you are not a French citizen M Sarkozy can have you deported—very quickly. We need to re-establish that kind of respect here for the office of our Home Secretary.

But most importantly, their intelligence analysis has proved to be more cutting edge than ours. Their *Renseignements Generaux* (literally General Information, roughly the equivalent of Special Branch in the UK), the second and more grass-roots domes-tic French intelligence agency appears, as mentioned earlier, to have believed in a formal assessment that a bomb plot would emerge from the UK Pakistani community soon. This is exactly what happened on 7 July.

The *Renseignements Generaux* keep a close eye on everyone of interest to the authorities in France—especially in Paris. We immediately imagine undercover agents spying without their subjects knowing it. There is that, too, of course. The French President is said to receive a report each day on the various goings on in the city of Paris. President Mitterand famously and scandalously used the *RG* to keep a discreet eye on the various starlets he had his eye on and would take close notice of their various rival romantic entanglements. So they say. But in fact, most the information of the *Renseignements Generaux* is gathered by maintaining open contacts. Nowadays the daily report is as likely to concentrate on the mood and intentions in the various Islamic suburbs of Paris.

It means that the French know exactly at any time what is going on in the various arrondissements of Paris, down to the Islamist bookshop that is not paying its full taxes. It is information that may not of itself be immediately useful, but what it allows the French to do is to pick up on the slightest fluctuations in mood and gives early warning of trouble ahead.

One wonders what its agents would have made of Beeston, the plotters' home ground. For instance, the service has operated a (controversial) clandestine opinion polling capability since 1964. It is able to put together usually accurate estimates of the political intentions and allegiances of arrondissements or smaller areas of Paris and elsewhere in France. Previously much concerned with student disaffection or irredentist former colonists from Algeria, the *RG* now pays close attention to France's Islamic communities and is usually able to pinpoint centres of disaffection and extremism—early. Replicating this system in the UK would allow us to direct our intelligence and security resources to much greater effect.

As part of understanding our current intelligence needs better we urgently have to review all our existing relationships.

Our intelligence services are at the moment organised like our armed forces—to support the foreign policy of the United States. But why is it a given that we should devote so much time and effort to sustaining this relationship in which we are the junior partners? It supplies us with world intelligence, but to what end? What we really need at the moment is backyard or European intelligence. Such intelligence may be better supplied and compared with our European neighbours.

There is a sense which goes throughout the Iraq crisis of 'punching above our weight'. It is commonly said to be the benefit of our transatlantic relationship. But do we really need to be a world intelligence power any longer, particularly as it may not benefit us in any real sense? When our threats are local why not be a European intelligence power—where we devote time and effort to our own security rather than getting stuck into trouble abroad?

# 5

# The Iraqi War

## Politics

*The reliability of intelligence assessments is important not just for the success of the country's external policy, but also for the confidence held by internal constituencies in the correctness of the government's judgement. (The impact of any proven bias in British intelligence assessments on Iraq would hardly be helpful, for instance, in rallying the UK's own moderate Islamic community to support the anti-terrorism effort.)*[8]

Have attitudes to Iraq contributed to the danger?

Yes of course, they have.

Opposition to the war in Iraq does not equate with terrorism but it has strained loyalties, and not just amongst our Muslim communities. Muslim fanatics were always fanatical—no concession is ever going to appease them whether they are British fanatics or foreign fanatics. It's not that they are mad in a psychological sense, it is just that they have an ultimate aim that is non-negotiable. Each concession fuels their appetite further in that they regard the concession merely as a staging post to the ultimate aim. By extension, such people would simply view Iraq as another string to their fanatical bow. It proves their point, as they see it—yet again: the West wants to conquer the Middle East and reduce the influence of Islam.

But reasonable people of all faiths and communities have, too, been split away by the war from the mainstream consensus. Wars may be necessary—but they upset people seriously. You may by due process declare war on behalf of the British people, but because of the death, pain and suffering involved that does not mean everyone will promptly fall in line behind your decision. It is here that you run a risk. The best intelligence system is everyone who is on your side—and that includes crucially the population at large. You do not want anger about the process to have a corrosive effect on the level of cooperation you need.

One should, perhaps for the record, declare one's hand when speaking about Iraq—precisely because it is such an emotive issue. I was at the time of the invasion of Iraq on 19 March 2003 an enthusiastic supporter of the war—and remained so even after it became apparent that the intelligence books had been 'cooked'—'subconsciously' at least if you were convinced by Lord Hutton's immortal phrase. There were and remain good arguments for intervention in Iraq although all of them are subject to a success test. You can get away with it if it works—if it does not you run into trouble.

The real reason for UK military action remains opaque—there have been too many versions given to us. But I am sure that even if the means used to justify it to the people were inappropriate the motivation was respectable enough. What I did not know at the time was that our principal military ally in Iraq had no plan for a properly conducted occupation and that the UK had failed to prepare proper intelligence assessments on the likely trajectory of stability and opposition to the occupation. The tragedy of the Anglo-American intervention in Iraq is therefore in my view not that it was illegal but that—with more forethought and better analysis—it could have worked.

I still think it was a perfectly reasonable option to have gone to war in Iraq acknowledging as the JIC did in 2003 that it would increase the threat to our country from terrorism, provided that we had some goal in mind that in the longer term would improve our security and provided that proper measures were put in place to protect us in the meantime. Nor do I have a problem with the Presidency of George W. Bush. During my two and a half year secondment to the Cabinet Office I was probably the only person in the building who wanted George Bush to win the 2000 presidential election and predicted to my colleagues that he would win handsomely. He has proved a disappointment although there is much still to admire about him.

To get back to the discussion at hand, it is irrelevant whether personally one feels the war was a good, a bad or an ugly decision when assessing the security risk the war created. We are looking at the possible effects on the terrorist threat at home of our intervention in Iraq and the implications of the intervention for the collection and analysis of intelligence for our home security. Given that it happened and a decision to go to war is more often than not divisive, the question is what can we reasonably expect our government to anticipate in intelligence terms and put in place for our protection and security. Did and does the system work? Was and is enough being done to cope with the fall-out from such a decision?

In a situation of national stress, accurate government information comes at a premium, and the same of course applies to the government being seen to supply credible information. As we know from the Hutton and Butler inquiries, political pressure on the intelligence apparatus created precipitous distortions on what might otherwise be considered facts.

Embarrassingly, the government's unwillingness or inability to act straightforwardly on this matter has now become a highly damaging contributing factor to our weakened security. Its failure to admit that involvement in Iraq has led the UK into danger—despite the well known views of the Joint Intelligence Committee (JIC) at the start of the war and the since leaked views of the head of the foreign office—has created a major propaganda opening for Al Qaeda sympathisers. They have made this abundantly clear in their ghoulish broadcasts since 7 July—one appended to Siddique Khan's 'living will' (more properly his confession that he intended to murder) on Al-Jazeera. It was and remains a severe mistake by the government, and we cannot undo the harm these tapes and similar propaganda have caused and will cause.

As our political leaders seem unable publicly to embrace a reality of their actions, one must also raise questions about their internal capacity for facing these issues. The matter has become live by their omission.

There are a series of questions we need answered insofar as it is possible to do so without betraying secret information that could prejudice our security operations—that means information that should genuinely remain secret, rather information that might prove embarrassing. Did the intelligence services warn the government that our security situation would deteriorate at least in the short term as a result of intervening in Iraq? Have there been any further warnings about a deterioration in security in the UK by the JIC or JTAC since the start of the war in Iraq? What was done about these? Is it even possible given the fraught atmosphere to produce an intelligence assessment that looks properly at Iraq? Is MI6 able to direct its efforts properly there and come to a true understanding of the realities on the ground and their implications for us and our armed forces? After all Mr Scarlett the current chief of the Secret Intelligence Service or 'C' as he is know by long custom is hardly a detached and clinical observer of events in Iraq—he supervised production of the dodgy 24 September dossier which gave rise to both the Hutton and Butler inquiries.

The invasion of Iraq may not have been the cause of the attacks on 7 July—to understand that is too broad a subject for here and would involve too much history to be of practical use at this stage. And it is not clear what role Iraq played in the radicalising of the individual suicide bombers. You would need a psychologist and perhaps a theologian to explain it.

It is possible that British intervention in Iraq or rather a highly one-sided and propagandised version of it was the factor which tipped Siddique Khan over the top. Personally I doubt it. He was probably the kind of fanatic that was coming for us anyway and would have found some other excuse, some other embroidered cause to attack his fellow countrymen. I have seen many like him in Northern Ireland. Some have a dangerous charisma but most build off not just the charisma but an atmosphere of menace with which they are able to intimidate the community.[9]

But Iraq straddles the two enabling factors—mirror images of each other—which made the attacks easier to plan and press home.

The first is that the war and occupation of Iraq are widely seen by many in this country (of all faiths and communities) as illegal and unjust. Many British Muslims would appear to have taken this view if the popular demonstrations at the time and more recently are anything to go by. This does not make them supporters of terrorism but these strongly held views amounting no doubt in several areas to a strong hatred of the government over this subject have given the fanatics their opportunity. Suddenly their views have a resonance and grounding in reality which gives them the confidence and opportunity to reach out to new recruits. It is more difficult to put up a reasonable argument against them. Terrorists require a pool of sympathisers to sustain them and to a certain extent validate them. It is very difficult to kick off or sustain a terrorist movement where there is no sympathy at all. Sympathisers come in all types along the spectrum—active supporters, fellow travellers right up to the mildest but most dangerous type of all—those willing or forced to turn a blind eye—the most numerous and the most likely to see sense or suspect something.

Second, the position of mainstream Islam has been weakened by inaction with implications for both intelligence and security. Terrorists wish to restrict the flow of information to the authorities. This is easily achieved in communities with historical antipathies to the mainstream as in Northern Ireland—for long historical reasons as I have described above. No doubt blunders were made by the army and the security forces which made it easier. It is testament to the neglect approaching negligence in the UK that the information restriction has been achieved without these dramas. The point is not that Iraq radicalises the likes of Siddique Khan it is that it gives them the space to operate.

Unfortunately with Iraq it is not just that many people view the war as unjust and illegal—but they believe that it was based on a lie. In other words the enabling atmosphere for Islamist terrorism feeds off the way we went to war as well as the perceived nature of the war itself. The intelligence scandals could not have been designed better to cause offence, disaffection and alienation among not just the Muslim community but anyone who might honestly have opposed the war.

There was genuine disagreement over the war even amongst military types who could normally be expected to fall into step once the decision had been made to commit the armed forces to action. We know that the JIC, even at a time when it was producing assessments to order, sexed-up to support the case for war in Iraq, retained enough independence and backbone to produce an assessment warning that our involvement in Iraq would increase the threat of terrorism. This may have referred only to the prospect of a terrorist threat from overseas. We know from a leaked letter by Sir Peter Jay that the head of the foreign office was warning that the UK's foreign policy was alienating our own Muslim population. The opposition increased exponentially once the various intelligence sleights of hand became public. One can only guess what the level of opposition must have been like in a closed or partially closed British Muslim community. It is a political question more than an intelligence one but the mechanics of going to war next time (if there is a next time) will prove much more complicated than merely arranging a vote in the House of Commons or commissioning the appropriate legal advice.

It is a curious phenomenon in the modern world where few people expect much of politicians that we expect them to tell the truth on matters of intelligence and security—or if they cannot and the government is entitled to its secrets—that they are economical with the truth in a way that protects national security rather than enhances political advantage or attempts to justify a particular policy. This did not happen in the run up to the Iraq war. The very fundamentals of analysis including the raw intelligence on which it was based were interfered with and we are now reaping some of the unintended consequences. The depressing irony is that cooking the intelligence books may well be one of the causes of our current difficulties—and one of the most powerful tools we have against terrorism are our intelligence and analytical services—compromised by this cavalier approach.

★ ★ ★

Given these mistakes and the increased risk of attacks they have caused, it is necessary to regain the trust of the entire population in Britain. It seems an organisational overhaul is long over due. But one vital ingredient will be increased transparency. Official policy is currently not to trouble the public with threat levels and alerts, unless there are specific measures that they can take to reduce the threat. I am sure the public at large would rather know the current threat/alert state than feel they are being patronised. Warnings should be made much more available to the public—probably by a recognised spokesman. If our banking and industrial enterprises and other key parts of our national infrastructure are given information, this should be supplied publicly as well—via an ombudsman or via a website.

Overall spending on counter-terrorism at government level was one billion in the year of September 11. It was 1. 5 billion pounds last year and will be 2. 1 billion by 2007-8. Ken Livingstone estimated the figure spent in London on training and equipment for the immediate response to an attack (specifically a multiple attack on the tube—though not apparently on official communication lines inside the tube) ran into tens of millions of pounds.[10] These are enormous amounts of money. The tax payer may not have got the best deal in exchange, but what is most worrying is that there seems little prospect of change as the government does not seem to think it can do any better.

# Conclusion

# The New Strategic Reality

Let us be clear. No responsible person or politician is 'soft on terror', except those that sympathise with terrorism. The efforts and manoeuvres of pundits and politicians to paint the other party or the other side as somehow soft on terror are dishonest and underhand. We should assume that views held across the spectrum of society on the causes of terrorism, or on the case for civil liberties, are honestly held—and that the individual or group holding those views believe they are making a proper contribution to the argument on how we can make ourselves safer.

It does not mean that all views are equally valid or likely to be equally effective. But it does mean that they can be publicly tested in argument without being closed down as 'soft on terrorism.'

Some suggest in the case of catastrophe that it is

unfair to second-guess hard working officials under the sledgehammer pressures of modern media and government decision cycles. Having been a government official, I agree that it is sometimes a little unfair. An attack on the benefit of hindsight wielded by commentators can be a legitimate defence.

And there are other powerful reasons that counsel us to tread carefully when criticising a response to terrorism or the measures we have in place to deal with it. There is the central problem that the purpose of modern terrorism is to turn us against each other. After Madrid it is clear that this kind of terrorism also has a specifically political purpose—to turn us against our governments. We have to take this into account, too.[11]

Obviously if we had known what was going to happen on 7 July we would have acted differently. 'If only I had known' is one of the major leitmotifs of the human condition.

But a cool and clear understanding of a threat is essential to putting in place defensive measures. Criticisms using hindsight are therefore perfectly valid. It involves an attempt to break away from the dead hand of complacency. Regardless of any political calculation we are perfectly entitled to examine the security policy of any government and make a judgement as to whether it can be organised better. It is one of the standard tools in our analytical armoury.

★ ★ ★

So far and tragically we have lost over 90 soldiers, sailors and airmen doing their duty in Iraq—and now 52 on the home front. To use American slang from the Vietnam era—that's a good kill ratio for the Al Qaeda franchise.

The real killer likely to emerge from Iraq is what analysts call 'blowback'—shorthand for the likely diaspora of terrorist know-how and motivation from Iraq in the future. This will happen regardless of whether Iraq stabilises or not in the coming months. The savage insurgency has lasted long enough to spawn some charismatic monsters that have pitted themselves principally against the US forces with some success. A mark of the development of a number of insurgent groups in Iraq is their aggressiveness and the continuing improvisation of their tactics. Iraq may not just have been a radicaliser—it may also be the best training ground there is. In fact it is almost an ideal training ground. The American Army is highly effective when present in force but unable to maintain sufficient combat troops on the ground to accomplish more than local and temporary superiority. Air power has its uses but in the counter-terrorist role needs high grade real time intelligence which is not consistently available.

7 July was mercifully a smaller scale attack than 9/11—but it was carried out by Britons prepared to

kill their fellow countrymen in the cause of jihad. Further interventions in the Middle East or elsewhere by UK armed forces are likely to run the risk of a terrorist response on the UK mainland. The new strategic reality is not that Al Qaeda's operational reach extends into the heart of the west but that it does not have to. The message from the men in hiding on the Pakistan/Afghanistan border or possibly somewhere on the Horn of Africa is not 'we can attack you' but rather 'we can persuade your own people to attack you'. The days when we could settle down in comfort with a beer and watch the spectacular results of the latest high-tech bombardment of our or Uncle Sam's enemies far away secure in the knowledge that the only people in danger were our troops at the front— are over. El Alamein marked the end of British military autonomy. Baghdad and Basra will mark the end of our military role as younger brother of the US.

In a sense we have come full circle—future wars undertaken by the UK on our own account or as an agent of the United States will not be possible unless they attract strong support—across our multi-cultural community. This is what multi-cultural Britain means. The old instinctive support for the United States may no longer be there. Attitudes to aerial bombardment have changed. Bomber Harris was a hero to the wartime generation but modern day sensibilities about bombing are different—not only on ethnic or religious lines. Many people are uneasy about the massive use of air power to win wars. There is something inherently unfair about it. And even if well controlled, well directed and well delivered as most Anglo-American air raids were innocent people get killed. Even if that is justified in some eyes it offers the malicious propagandist priceless material.

There will probably be further attacks in the UK by Britons and others in the cause of Islamist extremism. There is still just enough sympathy for the cause and enough intimidation in place to give particularly lower-level terrorists enough operational space to have a reasonable chance of mounting successful attacks. The bureaucratic and ideological frictions within our security system will help the terrorist for now but we, I hope, are about to become more formidable in the homeland security sphere.

The threat will be especially acute at the point when we quit Iraq. Whether we scuttle or leave the place in reasonably good order does not matter in the short term. Hard-core, very hard-core Islamist terrorists who have won their spurs in Iraq will wish to turn their attention either in the bitterness of defeat or in the exultation of partial victory against their enemies in the West. In this case the UK will be in danger but will be well positioned to defend herself—we are after all still an island. It will be much easier for us to control who comes and who goes from these islands—if we want to. Provided we are vigorous and energetic and manage to cast off some of the odd ideas which seem to permeate our security system—our chances of thwarting them will improve. If we seek to preserve Londonistan or the covenant of security we are lost. I hope that we do not have to wait for another attack to get it right.

# Endnotes

1  *Observer* on Sep 4 2005.

2  Iraq's Weapons of Mass Destruction: The Assessment of the British Government, http://www. fco. gov. uk/Files/kfile/iraqdossier. pdf.

3  13 September, House of Commons Home Affairs Committee.

4  *Ibid.*

5  *Ibid.*

6  Neither strategy works where the suicide bombs work on the dead man's handle principle where it is the release of, for example, a finger or lever and not the application of pressure that detonates the device. British Army grenades, as every schoolboy knows, work on this principle. Some of the latest and most sophisticated suicide bombs are detonated remotely by a mission commander stood back from the target location.

7  13 September, House of Commons Home Affairs Committee.

8  Black, Crispin in *Business and Security*, Bailes and Frommelt eds, The Stockholm International Peace Research Institute—Oxford University Press 2004, pp 179-180.

9  Think intimidation rather than Islam. We know and understand the effects of 'why is there not a Sinn Fein sticker in your window'? With our background in Northern Ireland we understand only too well the epidemiology of intimidation. We know full well from our own recent military and

political history how whole communities can be turned against us by a few strongmen using intimidation to build on perceived grievances and how whole communities can be corrupted by a few or at least turned into places where no one sees anything, no one reports anything to the police and everyone has to turn a blind eye.

10   13 September, House of Commons Home Affairs Committee.

11   One must be careful not to portray the bombers as more skilled than they really are. Did the Madrid plotters really expect the government of the day to lose the election? If the bombs had been blamed directly on Al Qaeda early—and many experts shared the view that it was ETA—the outcome would have been different. It was the appearance of dishonesty by the Spanish government that did for them.

# Index

95